FACING YOUR FEARS

FACING YOUR FEARS

A NAVY SEAL'S GUIDE TO COPING WITH FEAR AND ANXIETY

DON MANN
WITH KRAIG BECKER

Skyhorse Publishing

Skyhorse Publishing books may be purchased in bulk at special discounts
for sales promotion, corporate gifts, fund-raising, or educational purposes.
Special editions can also be created to specifications. For details, contact
the Special Sales Department, Skyhorse Publishing, 307 West 36th Street,
11th Floor, New York, NY 10018 or
info@skyhorsepublishing.com.

Skyhorse® and Skyhorse Publishing® are registered trademarks of
Skyhorse Publishing, Inc.®, a Delaware corporation.

Visit our website at www.skyhorsepublishing.com.

10 9 8 7 6 5 4 3 2

Library of Congress Cataloging-in-Publication Data is available on file.

Cover design by Brian Peterson

Print ISBN: 978-1-5107-4574-2
Ebook ISBN: 978-1-5107-4577-3

Printed in China.

CONTENTS

PART I

IDENTIFYING YOUR FEARS

In October of 1983, a dispute between two factions of the People's Revolutionary Army broke out on the tiny island nation of Grenada. The PRA had ruled the country for more than four years, but over that time disagreements had arisen within the party over who was best equipped to govern the nation moving forward. Those disagreements eventually led to violent clashes that resulted in dozens of deaths, including the ritual execution of the former party leader and seven of his closest allies.

As the turmoil continued to escalate, the streets of the Caribbean nation became a battleground, with members of the PRA waging war against each other. Innocent civilians found themselves caught in the crossfire as the situation went from bad to worse. What started as an internal struggle within the leading political party quickly shifted to a dangerous situation that endangered the lives of hundreds of people.

Amongst those living on the island at the time were 600 American medical students who attended

St. George's University. As Grenada descended into chaos, fear over the safety and whereabouts of those students began to grow back home in the US. With the Iran Hostage Crisis of 1980 still fresh in the minds of many Americans, President Ronald Reagan authorized military action in the Caribbean. The goal was to both quell the fighting and ensure the safety of the students and their families.

On October 25, the US military launched Operation Urgent Fury using forces from the Army, Navy, Air Force, and Marines. The plan was to launch a multi-pronged assault on the island, overwhelming the local forces as quickly as possible, while capturing strategic targets along the way. Naturally, the Navy SEALs were tasked with some of the most challenging and risky objectives of the entire mission.

Prior to the start of the military action, members of SEAL Team Six were ordered to perform reconnaissance on a strategic beach that would play an instrumental role in the invasion. The first of those recon missions ended in tragedy with four members of the team drowning after being airdropped at sea. A second attempt to survey the island was also scrubbed due to poor weather conditions. Ultimately, that meant that the US forces were going in blind without having a real sense of the resistance they might face.

Eventually it was time for Operation Urgent Fury to get underway with US Rangers dropping from the sky onto the island. The Army units were charged with securing Grenada's two airports and the campus where the American students were housed. While they went to work on those objectives, however, Navy SEALs were given two very important tasks that were best suited for their particular training and skills.

The two missions that were assigned to the SEALs included securing the extraction of Paul Scoon, Grenada's governor general, and capturing a radio tower on the island. To accomplish those goals, the SEALs broke into two teams and set off to achieve the objectives they had been assigned.

Like their Army counterparts, the SEALs didn't have much intel to go on before they launched their respective missions. They knew the locations of the governor general's home and the radio tower, of course, but they weren't sure how large of an enemy force they would face, nor how well armed they might be. Still, they had their orders and as usual they were determined to accomplish the tasks at hand.

The first order of business was capturing the radio tower, which was used by the People's Revolutionary Army to spread leftist propaganda to the people of Grenada. The plan was for the SEALs to take control of the tower and convert it for use as a tool for psychological warfare. If the SEALs found that that wasn't possible, their secondary objective was to destroy the antenna altogether.

The mission began with a Blackhawk helicopter flying members of SEAL Team Six to the radio station, which was captured quickly and without resistance. Enemy forces soon got wind of the SEAL presence, however, and launched a counterattack on the station using armored personnel carriers and heavily-armed troops.

Poorly equipped to deal with that kind of firepower, the SEALs knew it was imperative that they complete their objectives and vacate the area as quickly as possible. The team destroyed the radio transmitter and made a hasty retreat, cutting their way through a nearby fence while under heavy fire. Eventually they eluded the PRA forces by escaping into the ocean and in true frogman fashion, swam out to US ships that were waiting just offshore.

Meanwhile, the SEAL unit charged with securing Paul Scoon also captured the governor general's mansion almost completely unopposed. The team fast-roped from a hovering Army helicopter and soon found themselves inside the building, securing their target in a matter of minutes. But like their teammates at the radio tower, they soon found themselves under heavy fire as a fierce counterattack came their way. Before they had time to respond, enemy armored personnel carriers took up strategic positions, trapping the SEALs inside.

To make matters worse, in their haste to get to the battlefield the SEALs inadvertently left their back-up communications system behind. With the batteries on their primary comms unit running low, the team found themselves without a way to call for support. In a moment of quick thinking, one of the SEALs used the governor general's home phone to place a call to the central command post and before long the team received some much-needed air support in the form AC-130 gunships and AH-1 Cobra helicopters.

Despite those airstrikes the Grenadian forces held their ground, laying siege to the mansion for more than twenty-four hours. During that time, the twenty-two SEALs who had embarked on the mission were forced to hold their position and wait for help to arrive. That made for a long, tense night with heavy weapons fire being exchanged by both sides. Eventually however, US forces closed in on the mansion, defeated the enemy forces outside, and liberated the Navy SEALs, as well as Governor General Scoon.

All told, Operation Urgent Fury lasted just three days, but during that time US forces eliminated not only the leftist forces that controlled Grenada, but a cadre of Cuban troops and advisors that were stationed there, too. All of the American medical students were eventually accounted for and secured as well, with the overthrow of the PRA eventually leading to the installation of a democratically-elected government.

"

The brave man is not he who does not feel afraid, but he who conquers that fear."

—Nelson Mandela

While the invasion of Grenada involved every branch of the US military, Navy SEALs served at the tip of the spear from the outset. The elite warriors were called upon to conduct early reconnaissance missions to determine enemy troop strength and positioning. Later they were given the most daring and dangerous objectives of any of the American troops, as well, being tasked with completing highly specialized objectives.

As with any large-scale military operation, things didn't always go as planned. But thanks to their top-notch training and high level of professionalism, the SEALs that were a part of Operation Urgent Fury were able to maintain their focus and complete the missions they were assigned. Even as heavily-armed enemy forces closed in on their positions, the SEALs remained disciplined and determined, achieving their objectives despite unexpected challenges.

That isn't to say that the SEALs didn't experience moments of uncertainty and fear. The members of Team Six who had captured the radio tower were vastly outgunned and heavily outnumbered, which would be enough to give even the most experienced and well-trained operatives a reason to take pause. But their training allowed them to control that fear and constructively channel it towards completing their mission. After destroying the communications antenna, they were also able to make good on their escape, slipping away into the ocean and leaving their pursuers behind.

Similarly, the SEALs that found themselves trapped inside the governor general's mansion for more than twenty-four hours faced moments of fear and uncertainty as well. They were up against overwhelming enemy forces, lacked a method of communicating with central command, and weren't sure when they could expect support to arrive. Yet they too held their ground, creating a stalemate with PRA soldiers while patiently waiting for reinforcements.

There is a common misconception that Navy SEALs don't experience fear. In fact, quite the contrary is true, as fear is a normal, rational human emotion that most of us experience at various times throughout our lives. How we rationalize and control that fear plays an important role in how we react to it, however. For some individuals, fear can be so paralyzing that they are unable to collect their thoughts or even make a move. For others, that same feeling of fear can create an adrenaline rush that spurs them into action, although the results of those actions aren't necessarily positive.

Whether you're a Navy SEAL or a civilian, identifying and acknowledging your fears, and learning to maintain focus and control, can be important skills to master. By understanding the impact that fear can have on you as a person, you can also examine the ways that you can manage it, channel your emotions, and potentially overcome it altogether.

Before identifying the fears that you have in your life, it is important to understand exactly what fear is. The Merriam-Webster dictionary defines fear as an unpleasant or upsetting emotion that is brought on by the belief that someone—or something—is dangerous and could cause us pain or harm. This describes the feelings that we might get when encountering a stranger after dark or coming across a snake on the trail while out for a hike. Those types of fears are brought on by something tangible, however, while many of our fears can end up being more abstract and harder to actually pinpoint.

For example, one of the most common fears

amongst both men and women is public speaking. Many of us shudder at the idea of actually getting up in front of a group of people and giving a speech or presentation. This can elicit very real and visceral feelings, causing our hands to sweat, our hearts to palpitate wildly, and an uncomfortable pit to form in our stomachs. But there is no real threat or danger that comes with public speaking, so what is it about that particular activity that makes us feel this way?

Studies show that other common fears include a mix of both the real and intangible. For instance, many people list fear of heights, darkness, and flying on their list of phobias. Others rank insects, needles, and sharks. Some of those things do indeed pose an actual threat of physical harm, while others aren't especially threatening at all. Darkness, for example, isn't particularly dangerous in and of itself, but it does provide the ability to mask something that could potentially cause harm. An overactive imagination can automatically fill in the details, stirring up thoughts and feelings that induce fear, even when there isn't necessarily any reason to be afraid.

Often times the fears that we identify are not necessarily the same as the ones that we actually feel. In the case of public speaking, for instance, the sense of dread that we get isn't about standing up in front of a group of people and talking to them about a certain subject but is instead deeply rooted in something else. We might worry that we'll end up looking foolish or not come across as knowledgeable as we'd like. We might be self-conscious about how we look or worry about boring our audience. The point is, the actual act of public speaking isn't probably what we fear at all, but instead we worry about the potential consequences of what *could* happen while we're standing in front of others.

"

Being brave isn't the absence of fear. Being brave is having fear but finding a way through it."

—Bear Grylls

Fear is often generated simply by thinking about all the possibilities of things that might happen to us, even if they aren't all that likely to actually happen. For example, we're afraid of flying because we have images of airplane crashes seared into our psyche. Similarly, many of us are afraid of sharks because we've seen the movie *Jaws*. Director Stephen Spielberg used tension—not to mention the film's iconic soundtrack—to create a sense of dread that managed to jump off the screen and stay with us in a very real way.

The truth of the matter is that statistically speaking flying remains the safest way to travel and only a handful of people actually experience a shark attack at any point in their lives. Unfortunately, we aren't always rational beings when it comes to our fears. Even though we can read numerous articles and reports that assure us that air travel and swimming in the ocean are completely safe, it can be difficult to convince our brains otherwise.

Learning to identify and acknowledge the things that we are afraid of is typically the first step in learning how to manage those fears. By taking ownership of the things that make us fearful, we're acknowledging that those fears, rational or not, do indeed exist. This can often be harder than we might expect in part because of yet another fear— the fear of appearing weak.

Deep, overwhelming fear can often leave us feeling helpless and vulnerable. Conversely, admitting that certain fears exist can result in similar feelings as well. By simply acknowledging that something strikes fear into our hearts, we often feel that we are not as strong, self-assured, or talented as we think we should be. That can be hard to admit to others and even more difficult to admit to ourselves.

The reality is that everyone has fears, including Navy SEALs. In fact, we're all born with a few instinctual fears already firmly in place. Loud noises will scare an infant, and a fear of heights seems to be instilled in most of us at birth, too. Those fears are meant to keep us safe at a young age when we're still learning about the dangers of the world around us. These natural fears provide us with a healthy dose of caution that keeps our innate curiosity in check for a time.

Most of the other fears that we come to know are learned or developed as we grow up. An encounter with an aggressive dog at a young age for example can cause us to avoid canines altogether as we get older. A fear of confined spaces—a.k.a. claustrophobia—may be the result of getting accidentally locked in a closet as a child. Those types of phobias are actually more common than you might expect and since their origins are directly related to very real events, they are often understandable and relatable.

While these types of fears can be terrifying and absolutely paralyzing at times, due to their unique nature, they don't tend to hold us back from achieving our goals in life. If you're afraid of dogs, you simply avoid encountering them whenever possible. If you find small spaces to be scary and suffocating, you'll usually go to great lengths to avoid those types of places. These phobias don't tend to have an impact on our day-to-day lives, and we learn to live with them as best we can. They may unexpectedly turn up from time to time, but for most of us, they don't impact us in a meaningful way when it comes to pursuing our larger goals.

However, there are still plenty of other fears that can get in the way of us finding success and achieving everything that we want out of life. These types of fears can be just as paralyzing in their own way, bringing on stress, indecision, and anxiety. Worst of all, we may not even consciously know that these fears even exist, which makes them even larger stumbling blocks than the ones that we already recognize and have learned to avoid.

One of the most common fears is the fear of failure. Most of us have goals for ourselves both professionally and personally, but often we end up stifling those dreams out of a fear of never being able to attain them. We're so afraid of failing that we don't even try to achieve the things we want, preferring to stay safely inside our comfort zones where we never have to risk anything at all. By playing it safe we do avoid the possibility of failure, but we also eliminate the chance of success at the same time.

There are few professions that face as high of stakes as that of a Navy SEAL. These men take part in some of the most dangerous and difficult military operations imaginable and more often than not, failure simply isn't an option. This drives a SEAL to train harder, plan and prepare more diligently, and bring precision and discipline to every aspect of his life. Fear of failure pushes these elite warriors to be the absolute best operators that they can possibly be. By constantly honing their skills and talents, a SEAL reduces the chances of failure in everything they do, be it training or conducting a raid.

The same can't be said for most other people, however, as a fear of failure is often at the root of the fears that hold us back. If you're one of the many who are afraid of public speaking, for instance, chances are that the root cause of that fear is the thought of failing in front of a crowd. Getting up in front of people and giving a speech or presentation isn't all that intimidating in and of itself, and in fact, it can be a real honor depending on the circumstances. But once again our imaginations can get the better of us, allowing self-doubt to erode our confidence. When that happens, we begin to question our own abilities, allowing the fear of failure to truly creep in.

The mind is a powerful tool that can work both for and against us. While it is true that fear can fill the imagination with negative thoughts, a disciplined and strong mindset can work the opposite way, as well. Being able to accurately identify and control our fears allows us to get past the obstacles that we create for ourselves within our own minds. The idea of speaking in front of others can be utterly terrifying if we allow it to be, but if we refuse to give those negative thoughts any power, we can push them aside and accomplish great things.

"

Nothing in life is to be feared, it is only to be understood. Now is the time to understand more, so we may fear less."

—Marie Curie

There are plenty of incredibly successful people who have left an indelible mark on history while still having an overwhelming fear of public speaking. For instance, Thomas Jefferson famously dreaded the thought of talking in front of crowds, so much so that he was often extremely quiet, even when interacting with small groups. Jefferson, who was the primary architect of the Declaration of Independence and one of the leading thinkers among America's Founding Fathers, eventually became the third president of the United States. During his two terms in office, he only ever gave two speeches in public, both of which were at his inaugurations. He even sent his annual State of the Union addresses to Congress in written form, preferring not to share his thoughts verbally.

In building a new nation, Jefferson found a friend and confidant in John Adams, with the two serving in the Continental Congress together. But even Adams seldom heard Jefferson speak remarking, "During the whole time I sat with him in Congress, I never heard him utter three sentences together." Adams would also describe his friend's oratory skills in the Senate as "prompt, frank, explicit, and decisive upon committees and in conversation."

Despite his crippling fear of speaking in public, Jefferson was nevertheless one of the most influential men in American history. He mastered the art of the written word and when he did give a speech in front of a group, he generally went for brevity and power rather than long-winded orations. No doubt this helped him to at least tolerate the times when he was required to address a crowd, but it also gave even greater weight to those rare occurrences when he expressed his thoughts and opinions aloud.

Jefferson isn't the only man who played a major role on the world's stage yet still harbored a fear of speaking in public. Mahatma Gandhi, the influential leader of the independence movement in India during the 1940s, shared the same dread of addressing crowds. So much so that Gandhi rarely spoke in public, even at small gatherings attended by friends. He simply didn't feel comfortable with the eyes and ears of others turned in his direction.

Once, while he was a law student in London, Gandhi was reportedly asked to speak in front of a group known as the "Vegetarian Society." He wrote a speech espousing the virtues of a meatless diet, but when it came time to share his thoughts with his peers, he simply could not get the words out. After uttering a single line, he panicked, lost his place, and went completely blank. The speech had to be read by one of the other members of the group, while an embarrassed Gandhi sheepishly sat nearby.

Eventually Gandhi would go on to become a powerful and well-respected public speaker, but like Jefferson, he was a man who came to understand the value of a few very powerful words. This revelation came as he took a leadership role in resisting British rule. As others rallied behind him, Gandhi realized that his own fears needed to be set aside for the greater good of his country. Helping to earn India's freedom ended up serving as his greatest motivation to get past his own personal challenges.

Later in life Gandhi was quoted as saying, "My hesitancy in speech, which was once an annoyance, is now a pleasure. Its greatest benefit has been that it has taught me the economy of words." Essentially, he turned a weakness into a strength and became one of the most inspiring figures of the twentieth century, leading a nonviolent revolution that continues to inspire others more than seventy years after his death.

"

Do not fear mistakes.
You will know failure.
Continue to reach out."

—Benjamin Franklin

When it comes to identifying the roots of a phobia like a fear of public speaking, being able to honestly and accurately evaluate your own strengths and weaknesses plays a crucial role. We don't always like to look too hard at ourselves, preferring to search for answers in external sources instead. It is so much easier to blame other individuals or forces beyond our control for our own shortcomings, as it provides an excuse as to why we are unable to reach our goals.

Thoughtful self-reflection forces us to confront things about ourselves we may not like to admit, which can clear the path to achieving the things we want in life.

This ability to self-evaluate plays an important role throughout the career of a Navy SEAL. In order to continually improve his existing skills, while still learning new ones, a SEAL must be able to accurately identify where his training and experience is lacking and then address those gaps. In this way, he is constantly working on becoming a better warrior and teammate.

By accurately and honestly assessing his own skillset, a SEAL is also accepting responsibility for identifying his own deficiencies and finding ways to eliminate them. He doesn't blame his lack of knowledge or physical preparation but is instead proactive when it comes to finding ways to becoming a better Navy SEAL. In doing so, he knows that the responsibility for achieving his personal goals, and those of his team, falls squarely on his own shoulders.

That same level of personal accountability plays a crucial role when it comes to evaluating our own fears. Being able to accurately identify the things that frighten us, and take ownership of them, can go a long way towards putting our phobias behind us. This is an important step towards achieving the things we want out of life. Left unaddressed, those same fears will continue to be the stumbling blocks that prevent us from progressing towards our goals, weighing us down like an anchor.

Fear of failure is one of those phobias that can take on many forms. We've already talked at some length about how an aversion to public speaking likely has its roots in fear of failure, but there are plenty of other ways that it can manifest itself in an effort to trip us up. For example, an athlete who is afraid of injury or making a mistake on the playing field may actually be masking a fear of failure instead. This can lead to a tentative performance, which can ultimately make the fear of failure a self-fulfilling prophecy.

Avoiding that pitfall is the key to being successful in just about any venture. As human beings, we often have the uncanny ability to sabotage our own efforts simply because we can't manage to get out of our own way. This can make failure seem like an inevitability when the truth is that had we been honest with ourselves and taken the proper steps to overcome our fears, we could have stayed on course and achieved whatever it was we set out to do.

One of the forms of self-sabotage that comes along with a fear of failure is a complete lack of action in any form. In other words, because we are so afraid that our efforts will end in failure no matter what we do, we don't even bother trying at all. In a way, this is a form of self-preservation, as we look to avoid the possibilities of defeat at the expense of even taking a chance at victory.

The self-evaluation process can play an important role in this area as well. At some point, we have to ask ourselves, *how badly do we want to achieve the goals that we've set* and *how much we are willing to risk along the way?* By better understanding those questions, we also gain a better understanding of ourselves.

The old adage of "nothing ventured, nothing gained" has never been more accurate, meaning that if we want to be more successful in business, athletics, or life in general, we have to be willing to get off the couch and actively pursue the things we want most. Yes, there is a chance that we could fail, but at least we've given it a try, and that is far better than always wondering what we could have accomplished had we applied ourselves.

As debilitating as fear of failure can be, fear of success can be equally paralyzing. The idea of being afraid of actually succeeding at something seems counterintuitive, and yet it is a very real phobia for many. What makes it so much harder to overcome, however, is that even through very honest self-evaluation, it can still be extremely difficult to identify and navigate our way through that fear.

The idea behind this type of phobia is that success brings change, and that change can lead to significant upheaval and uncertainty in our lives. If we fail, we can easily retreat back to our comfort zone and we might even already have contingency plans in place to do just that. But if we succeed, we're heading down a path that could potentially have a significant impact on our lives, altering it in unforeseen ways forever. This can lead to uncertainty, which can be incredibly unsettling for some individuals.

A fear of success can manifest itself in numerous ways, many of which make it difficult to identify. For instance, those who are consciously or unconsciously afraid of the responsibilities and changes that come with being successful will often find ways to actively avoid doing the work that is necessary to reach their goals. They may talk about the things they are eventually going to do, but not focus on actually doing them. They are easily distracted by insignificant things that don't hold much importance or they could have a tendency to be indecisive, often second-guessing their own decisions and plans. In other words, those who have a fear of success can be just as adept at self-sabotage as those who fear failure.

Someone who has a fear of success may also

create their own obstacles by setting extremely high—almost unattainable—standards for their work. While striving for perfection is often seen as a positive trait, it can also serve as a crutch to keep us from moving forward instead. Perfectionists have a tendency to reject individual elements of a project that don't live up to their expectations, forcing additional revisions where they might not truly be needed. This is a way of slowing down progress and potentially delaying or eliminating their success altogether.

If you recognize some of these characteristics in your own behavior then perhaps it is time to ask yourself, *are you afraid of actually being successful*? If you struggle with the thought that reaching your goal could alter your life dramatically, or bring on stress-inducing responsibilities, then you may indeed find success to be a truly frightening proposition. This can lead to us unconsciously finding ways to prevent ourselves from reaching our goals or at the very least delaying any meaningful progress towards them.

Success can lead to a lot of complications. It can create a spotlight that we don't necessarily feel comfortable in and it can lead to new, unexpected challenges and responsibilities. Perhaps most daunting of all is the expectations that come along with success. If you're a successful athlete, you're expected to keep winning. If you're successful in business, you're expected to keep growing profits and expanding your customer base. The mere thought of those weighty expectations is enough to send some people retreating back into their comfort zone where they aren't required to push their personal boundaries in any way. Playing it safe means not having to deal with high expectations, but it also means never realizing your full potential.

Vincent van Gogh is one of the most famous and influential artists of all time, creating visually stunning works of art that continue to inspire generations of painters that have come after him. Today, when one of his works goes up for auction, it usually commands a hefty price, selling for tens of millions of dollars. Believe it or not, however, Van Gogh was actually plagued with a fear of success and the attention, responsibility, and expectations that it could bring him.

The Dutch artist told his family that fame was

a frightening prospect. He felt it was much easier to toil in obscurity, working on the paintings and drawings that pleased him personally rather than trying to appeal to a larger audience. Van Gogh thought that his work would suffer under the scrutiny that comes with a larger stage and a more public presence, so he was hesitant to sell his paintings or accept commissions for his work.

Because of this, van Gogh reportedly only sold a handful of paintings and drawings in his lifetime. In fact, *The Red Vineyards* is the only piece of art from the artist's catalog that is definitively known to have been sold while he was alive. As a result, when he committed suicide at the age of thirty-seven, van Gogh was practically penniless and not especially well known. He was the quintessential starving artist who felt uncomfortable with the thought of selling his art in order to make a living.

Today, the Dutch post-Impressionist is amongst the most beloved and revered artists of all time, with many of his paintings considered to be priceless masterpieces. Van Gogh's success came not long after his death when an appreciation for his works began to grow. Had he perhaps been able to manage his fear of success it is possible that he could have been more appreciated in his lifetime, possibly selling more of his art in the process.

"

It is impossible to live without failing at something, unless you live so cautiously that you might as well not have lived at all – in which case you fail by default."

—JK Rowling

Believe it or not, it is possible to have both a fear of success and a fear of failure at the same time. That's because the uncertainty and lack of confidence that both phobias bring to the table are often deeply rooted in the same part of our psyche. Many people feel that they aren't deserving of success or they lack the skills and talents to achieve it. Those are the thoughts that often fuel both types of fears, leading to indecision, procrastination, and other self-sabotaging behaviors.

Being afraid to both succeed and fail seems like a recipe for disaster, but in reality, it can be an indication of just how much someone wants to achieve their goals. These types of fears often manifest when we are obsessing about every detail that comes with reaching our objectives, including the possibilities that we'll come up short or be wildly successful. This can lead to an entirely different type of paralysis—one that leaves us questioning everything we thought we knew and each decision we make.

The simultaneous fear of success and failure isn't the only type of stumbling blocks that can hold us back from our goals, although it is among the most common. Other types of fears that can create formidable obstacles include fear of uncertainty, fear of change, and fear of rejection. Each of these can limit our ability to truly pursue our passions too, although they are often strongly linked to both success and failure.

A fear of uncertainty has been a primal human emotion for thousands of years. As a species, we have a natural predilection towards playing it safe and not venturing far out of our comfort zones. This is a survival instinct that is designed to keep us safe and secure, which also makes it a fear that we must often face if we hope to accomplish our goals.

For much of human history, uncertainty has surrounded our very lives. For thousands of years there were blank spots on the map and places just over the hill that we knew very little about. For millennia we stayed close to home, rarely venturing out into the larger world around us. Over time, however, our innate curiosity got the better of us, overcoming our fear of the unknown. This allowed us to begin to explore our surroundings, eventually sending intrepid men and women to the far corners of the globe simply because we wanted to know what was there.

Had we not been able to overcome our fear of uncertainty, explorers like Ferdinand Magellan would never have set sail around the world, charting the continents in the process. Nor would Marco Polo have ventured east in an effort to open trade routes between Europe and China. Overcoming our fear of uncertainty allowed American settlers to expand into the west, mountaineers to climb Mt. Everest, and astronauts to go to the moon. At one point, all of those things were considered dangerous and foolhardy, but had we allowed our fear to hold us back, we would have stayed stagnant as a species.

Most of us will never have the opportunity to embark on an epic expedition to explore remote and distant corners of the globe. Still, the fear of uncertainty remains an incredible obstacle that can prevent us from achieving our goals. Few things in life are ever certain and in order to accomplish big things we need to be able to take leaps of faith from time to time. By acknowledging your fear of uncertainty, you can also make the decision to put it behind you and embrace the unknown. For it is when we are in uncharted waters that we are going in search of our full potential.

"

Avoiding danger is no safer in the long run than outright exposure. The fearful are caught as often as the bold."

—Helen Keller

A fear of change can also prove to be a significant roadblock to success, keeping us locked safely inside our comfort zones while stifling the potential for growth. Typically, we fear change not because of change itself, but because we can't always predict the potential outcomes. Change in and of itself isn't necessarily a bad thing, but when we're unsure of exactly what form that change might take, we often end up choosing to play it safe in an effort to maintain our current position instead.

Not wanting the important elements in your life to change dramatically is natural, of course, particularly when you're already happy and content. But if you find yourself unwilling or unable to pursue your goals simply because you don't want to risk upsetting the apple cart, chances are you may be suffering from a fear of change.

Stepping outside your comfort zone means accepting change as a possibility and recognizing that the things you want to achieve are worth the risk. Change is a part of life and things rarely stay the same forever. Acknowledging and embracing that can make it easier to deal with changes as they come, rather than trying to avoid them altogether.

Finally, the fear of rejection is another phobia that can hold us back from achieving the things we want to accomplish. If you find yourself unable to share your ideas, pursue passion projects, or share your goals because you worry what others might think, you could have a fear of rejection. Oftentimes, this fear is a result of being criticized or ridiculed for our thoughts and beliefs in the past, which can lead to feelings of being isolated and alone.

A fear of rejection can prevent us from offering up our ideas or voicing our opinions simply because we're afraid that others might not agree with us. We all naturally want to fit in and be accepted, and sometimes that applies to the pursuit of our goals as well. If we share the idea we have for writing a book or creating a website, we might be told that that idea is a dumb one, making us feel self-conscious and foolish. As a result, we end up abandoning our personal or professional projects because we don't want to risk being ostracized.

The fear of uncertainty, change, and rejection are all closely related and are often intertwined with one another. In actuality, these phobias are just self-imposed walls designed to keep us safely inside our own comfort zones. If we stay in place, we don't have to risk anything of value, which means we'll never have to face the unknown or put ourselves in a position where we might fail or be rejected.

On the other hand, these types of fears are often amongst the most difficult to identify simply because we frequently avoid confronting them head on. Instead, we create a whole laundry list of excuses designed to let ourselves off the hook rather than actually accepting the fact that we might actually be afraid of something. Rather than admitting that we're scared of rejection, we simply tell ourselves that our ideas aren't ready to be shared and that we'll need to work on them longer before offering them to others. Instead of recognizing that we have a fear of change, we rationalize that we have too much to lose if we try to make a career shift, move to another part of the country, or start our own business. In our minds, these aren't necessarily seen as fears at all, but are instead rationalizations for why we shouldn't put ourselves out there.

The reality is, many of those rationalizations are just excuses that we've created to let ourselves off the hook. It is a self-preservation tactic that keeps us from confronting our true fears, but ultimately ends up holding us back. By identifying the true cause of those fears, we can begin to see the real meaning behind our excuses too. Understanding the root of our phobias can help to diffuse their power over us and allows us to make positive progress towards the things we truly want to accomplish.

Identifying the fears that create the obstacles to your success starts with acknowledging that those fears exist in the first place. Once you recognize that the things you are afraid of are potentially holding you back, you can begin to take inventory of your fears and examine the reasons why they have such a hold on you. In order to do that, however, you have to be prepared to be brutally honest with yourself.

This process requires a good deal of introspection and the ability to evaluate yourself accurately. Until you can honestly do that, you aren't really ready to confront your fears and begin the process of putting them behind you. Ultimately, that means that they will continue to weigh you down and hold you in place, preventing you from making any meaningful progress forward.

Fear is one of the most basic and shared human

emotions, and every one of us experiences it in some form from time to time. It can serve as an impediment to our progress or it can be turned into motivation to do great things depending on how you learn to deal with it. For a Navy SEAL, that often means being able to compartmentalize fear and channel into efficiency. During an operation, a SEAL can't afford to let fear become an impediment to the success of the mission, which is why it is vitally important that he be able to identify and control those feelings at all times.

Your objectives may not be the same as those of a SEAL, but you should still be able to pursue success with the same level of dedication and determination. That means that you don't ignore or deny your fears, but instead learn to explore and embrace them. When you can do that, you'll not only learn a lot more about yourself, but will discover ways to circumvent the things that have been holding you back. You'll also be ready to finally free yourself from those phobias altogether and start to explore everything that you are truly capable of.

PART II

EMBRACE THE FEAR

Fear is an incredibly powerful emotion, capable of generating a wide range of reactions. It has the ability to paralyze us in place or spur us to run further and faster than ever before. It can cause us to meekly retreat from confrontation or lash out with surprising strength and voraciousness. It can even prevent us from pursuing our goals or serve as a motivator that allows us to achieve significant accomplishments.

The first step in learning to face our fears is to properly identify exactly what we are afraid of, and perhaps discover the true cause of those feelings. Understanding how and why those phobias managed to manifest in our psyche can make it much easier to move past them. As already discussed, this process usually involves a deep and honest look at ourselves with the intent of finally putting our fright behind us.

Once we've managed to properly assess and diagnose the things that scare us, the next step in the process of facing our fears is to learn to manage them. In order to do that, we often need to embrace the things that frighten us the most and find a way to become more familiar with them. As with most things in life, further exposure can bring familiarity, which in turn can lead to our fears having much less of a hold on us.

Navy SEALs learn that the human mind is a powerful tool that can work both for and against us. Left to its own devices, our brains will create all kinds of scenarios that can lead to disaster, fueling the fears that we already have and potentially even creating new ones. In fact, that is one of the ways that our fears can go from things that we are madly concerned about to full-blown phobias that take over our lives.

On the other hand, a strong and disciplined mindset can allow us to control our fears and even potentially discover ways to make them work in our favor. Learning to channel our thoughts in a positive way can give us the ability to embrace fear, learn to live with it, and eventually release it altogether.

As part of SEAL training, SEALs learn to use visualization techniques to help them develop a stronger mindset. Visualization plays an important role in not just learning how to identify and control their fears but finding ways to channel them to achieve a specific outcome. Essentially, a SEAL runs through various aspects of an upcoming mission in his brain, considering all of the ways that things can go right and wrong. This allows them to explore the possibilities for success and failure ahead of time, while also creating a sense of familiarity with the operation.

When it comes time to conduct the mission, things don't seem quite so unfamiliar since the SEAL has already imagined various outcomes a dozen times over. This approach helps him to overcome any apprehension he might have simply by allowing his mind to consider how different variables could impact the operation. It also plays a pivotal role in developing those contingency plans in the event that something goes wrong.

"Do the thing you fear and the death of fear is certain."

—Ralph Waldo Emerson

This same process can be used in our lives to great effect as well. Visualization techniques have been shown to help athletes perform better in a competition and give entrepreneurs a leg up when pursuing their goals as well. It is a tactic that can also help students prepare more thoroughly for exams, business owners to chart a course for their company, and artists to envision their next performance or creation.

Athletes who have successfully used visualization techniques in order to compete include Olympic swimmer Michael Phelps, World Cup skier Lindsey Vonn, and basketball great Michael Jordan. Phelps has said that prior to a competition he would close his eyes and envision himself swimming the perfect lap, while Vonn would routinely prepare for an event by racing the course over and over in her mind. Reportedly, she would even lean back fourth into the curves, just as if she were already on her skies and heading down the hill.

As for Jordan, his visualization technique was a bit different and perhaps spurred on by his own fears. While in high school, he was actually cut from his basketball team as a sophomore. The impact of that event seemed to have left a lasting impression on him, because years later, even while playing in the NBA, he would envision his name on the roster to serve as motivation to train and play harder. The Hall of Famer has admitted that when he was tired and looking for an excuse to quit, he too would close his eyes and see his name listed in the line-up. That was enough for him to set aside his fatigue and push himself even harder.

Visualization has also proven to be extremely useful when it comes to controlling and embracing fear. As already mentioned, the fear of public speaking remains a major issue for many people, often ranking at the very top of the list in terms of the things that we admit to being afraid of. Usually, the stage fright that we experience before giving a presentation to a group of strangers is rooted in the fear we have of looking foolish or unprepared in front of people that we don't even know. But by visualizing ourselves successfully delivering our speech to a large crowd, we can anticipate what the experience will actually be like. We can imagine the layout of the room, the size of the stage, and even some of the faces in the audience. This allows us to rehearse our

presentation over and over again in our head, almost as if we've delivered the speech a dozen times
over. This can help reduce the amount of anxiety
and stress we feel before going on stage, making it
much easier to actually do the thing that we had
been dreading.

SEALs use the visualization technique as a re-
hearsal of sorts for both their training and missions,
continually thinking about the challenges they could
face and all of the things that could potentially go
wrong. That way, when they are sent out into the
field they can be more prepared for just about anything that could potentially happen. If the operation
should go awry for some reason, they've more than
likely already determined the best course of action
and can seamlessly shift to a well-thought-out contingency plan. In this way, they can minimize the
potential for disaster and control their own fear,
having already mentally prepared for the operation
to go off the rails.

This is yet another technique that we can adopt
and use to our advantage as well. One of the biggest
fears that we all have when taking on any ambitious
project—such as starting a business or planning a

major event—is that we won't actually be able to pull off our grand schemes. We worry that we aren't smart enough, talented enough, or hard working enough to actually achieve our objectives. We fear that we'll just end up looking like a massive failure in front of our friends, family, and coworkers.

But if we take a step back, carefully examine our plans, and look for potential areas of concern ahead of time, we can begin to consider all the ways that things could possibly go wrong. This gives us the opportunity to not only spot potential weaknesses in our plans ahead of time, it also provides us with the opportunity to come up with alternative options should we encounter an impasse along the way. In this way, we can learn to be more fluid with our approach to accomplishing our goals, rolling with adversity when it strikes, and more quickly shifting to another course of action if required.

By thinking about all of the potential problems that we could face, we are in a sense embracing our fear of failure. We're essentially admitting that our plans might not work out as well as we'd like them to, so we had better prepare for the consequences when things start to fall apart around us. And by developing contingency plans for when complications and unexpected challenges arise, we're preparing ourselves to handle those situations to the best of our abilities. As we recognize that failure is actually a part of the learning process on the road to success, we take away much of its power over us, greatly reducing our anxiety in the process.

Accepting the possibility of failure provides another positive benefit by often providing us with the courage we need to press forward in the pursuit of our goals. An overwhelming fear of failure can keep us rooted firmly in place, completely paralyzed and unable to take action towards our objectives. When that happens, we aren't able to achieve anything at all and our objectives remain out of reach. But when we're able to recognize that failure can play a vital role in helping us achieve the things we want, we can also move past the fears that have prevented us from making progress.

When you no longer allow thoughts of failure to dictate your actions, it can feel as if a tremendous weight has been lifted from your shoulders, allowing you to go after your goals with a greater sense of confidence and purpose. Failure is not a sign of weakness but can instead be a badge of honor that demonstrates our determination and focus.

If entrepreneurs like Elon Musk, Jeff Bezos, and Bill Gates hadn't been able to get past their fear of failure, we might not have companies like Tesla, Amazon, and Microsoft pushing the edges of innovation and technology. Had industrialists like Henry Ford and Andrew Carnegie stopped to consider their chances of failure, the advances they brought to the manufacturing process may have taken years or even decades to be introduced. But by not letting the fear of failure hold them back, these men have been able to change the world, creating new opportunities for many who have followed in their footsteps. And while all of them went on to be massively successful, in the early days that success was far from assured. In fact, failure was a very real possibility; yet they pursued their goals anyway.

For some people, the thought of failure doesn't induce a crippling fear that prevents them from pursuing their goals. Quite the opposite, in fact, as some individuals use that fear to feed their motivation instead. For these types of people failure simply is not an option and they will not accept anything less than giving everything they've got when it comes to completing their objectives.

This is a prime example of embracing a fear and using it to our advantage, turning something that frightens us into a competitive advantage instead. Those who are motivated in this way are often driven not so much by a fear of failure, but a fear of not succeeding, which on a fundamental level isn't the same thing. By doing this, our fears actually serve as fuel for our competitive fires, inspiring us to work, train, and prepare even harder.

Those who have a fear of not succeeding already believe they are on their way to accomplishing their goals, they just can't allow anything to prevent them from reaching them. Someone who is afraid of failing sees the obstacles in his or her path and decides to give up without even trying. The former sees opportunity, while the latter tends to see only adversity.

Where fear is, happiness is not."

—Seneca

NFL Hall of Famer Jerry Rice is the perfect example of an athlete who simply refused to allow fear of failure to hold him back. In high school he was an excellent wide receiver, but he didn't garner much in the way of attention from any big-name colleges or universities. Instead, he ended up playing at Mississippi Valley State where he went on to set a number of NCAA records while racking up impressive numbers in terms of yardage, catches, and touchdowns.

Rice's success in college did catch the attention of pro scouts, although some had concerns about his lack of pure running speed. That didn't faze the San Francisco 49ers, however, as they traded up in the first round of the 1985 NFL draft in order to take the wide receiver with the sixteenth pick. Some analysts thought the team had bet too much on Rice, pointing to the deficiencies in his athletic ability and the fact that he played at a small university as reasons for concern. Jerry took those criticisms in stride, however, and used them to motivate him to train and play even harder.

Throughout his career Rice's work ethic became the stuff of legend. Typically, he would begin the day with an intense cardio workout, running a five-mile route on the steep trails located near his San Francisco home. That workout would include ten 40-meter sprints up the steepest parts of that trail, causing his legs and lungs to burn with exertion. In the afternoon, he'd hit the weight room, spending hours doing equally intense intervals on a variety of weight machines. This was typically his schedule for six days a week across his entire career, which spanned more than twenty years. Most impressive of all was that this was his schedule during the off season, when most everyone else was relaxing and taking it easy.

During the season he brought that same intense work ethic to the team workouts, too. He would arrive in training camp already in tip-top shape and ready to go to work, even as other players struggled with their conditioning. In practice, whenever he caught a pass, he'd run the length of the field into the end zone every single time, only to sprint back to the huddle for the next play. Essentially, he refused to be out-hustled and took it as a personal challenge that he would be the hardest working man in the National Football League.

An example of this is a story told by San
Francisco quarterback and fellow Hall of Famer
Steve Young, who had the opportunity to witness
Rice's work ethic firsthand. In January of 1995, a
few days after the team had won the Super Bowl,
Young dropped by the 49ers training facility to collect a few personal belongings from his locker. As
he passed by the practice field, he spotted Rice running wind sprints and catching passes from one of
the groundskeepers. The past season had only just
ended and training camp was still seven months
away, and yet there was Jerry still constantly working on perfecting his skills.

Rice found motivation in the idea that others were quick to write him off even before he had
played a single down in the NFL. They were ready
to anoint him a failure simply because a stopwatch
said he wasn't as fast as the prototypical pro football player. That didn't just give him the motivation
he needed to earn a roster spot with the 49ers, it
also provided him with a burning desire to prove
the doubters wrong. He didn't set out to become
the greatest wide receiver the game has ever known,

that was simply a byproduct of all of his hard work, dedication, and absolute refusal to fail.

When he retired, Rice held nearly every significant career receiving record in professional football—and by a wide margin. His career number of touchdowns was 197—forty-one more than the guy in second place on the NFL's all-time list. With 1,549 receptions he had 300 more than the next closest player as well and his 22,895 receiving yards is nearly 7,000 more than anyone else. Along the way, Rice also won three Super Bowl rings and played in more games than any other player in league history who wasn't a kicker.

66

Fear has its use, but
cowardice has none."

—Mahatma Gandhi

Navy SEALs share many of the same motivations when it comes to training and preparation. Like Rice, they prefer to leave very little to chance and relish in the idea that no one works harder than they do. Their missions are some of the most difficult and demanding in the world, and generally leave little room for error. Because of this, SEALs are fond of saying "train as you fight, fight as you train." In other words, if you give it your all in training, and work to become the best at what you do, that will translate into success on the battlefield.

Knowing full well that failure comes with significant consequences, Navy SEALs push themselves to constantly improve their skills, talents, and physical conditioning. They know that when they are in the field they need to be as prepared as humanly possible, otherwise they aren't just letting themselves down, they are failing their teammates as well. This gives the "train as you fight, fight as you train" credo an even higher level of importance, as a potential failure can have devastating results. This is something that drives a SEAL throughout his entire career as he knows that if he doesn't do his job to the best of his abilities it can have dramatic and lasting consequences on his life and those around him.

Converting our fear of failure from a barrier to our success into a source of motivation means embracing that fear completely. Once again, by acknowledging the things that we are afraid of we can start to diffuse their power over us and channel that energy elsewhere. The result can be incredibly empowering, allowing us to shift our mindset away from being so afraid of failure that we can't even begin to try, to instead fearing what might happen if we don't try at all.

Learning to embrace our other fears can help us confront them too, even if they aren't quite as dramatic as a fear of failure. Many of us have common, day-to-day fears that can hold us back as well, keeping us locked away in the safety of our own comfort zones. Some of the most common fears, even amongst adults, include being scared of the dark or being afraid of heights. Others have a fear of talking to strangers or experience intense anxiety and fright when they have to travel by airplane.

Acknowledging that those fears exist in your life

is a good first step, but that alone won't help you overcome them. These fears will continue to hold sway over you until you decide to embrace and face them more directly. That means summoning up your courage and finding ways to put yourself in situations where you can experience the things that you are afraid of. As you gain that exposure you may start to find that the things that truly frightened you really aren't all that scary after all. At the very least, you're likely to learn how to manage and channel your fears more effectively.

In other words, if you have a fear of talking to strangers, you look for ways to put yourself into situations where you are forced to chat with people you don't know. Perhaps you join a book club or a hiking group filled with individuals you've never met before. The point is to get outside your comfort zone and begin to interact with new people. In this way, you can learn to get more comfortable with the idea of conversing with others you don't know, or at the very least start to feel more confident when meeting strangers for the first time.

Dealing with a fear of heights can be potentially more challenging, but the approach remains largely the same. Finding ways to safely expose yourself to high places can gradually allow you to embrace your fear and learn to manage it. This could involve joining a climbing gym, for instance, where you can slowly work your way up a climbing wall under your own power. This approach puts the control squarely into your hands, allowing you to expose yourself to as much or little height as you feel comfortable with at any given time. The important thing is that you get to set the pace while confronting the thing that scares you in a safe and supervised environment.

Other ways to deal with a fear of heights include standing on a balcony or climbing up a set of high stairs, then slowly approaching the edge to peer over to see what is below. This gives your mind and body the chance to adjust to the height and begin to feel secure with the environment. Over time, you can move to a higher vantage point and repeat the process, gradually gaining confidence and control. The process may not completely cure you of your fear, but it can give you the tools you need to at least manage it for brief periods of time.

This type of approach is known as immersion therapy, but the reality is that it is just another way to embrace your fears. The idea is to gradually expose someone to the things that they are afraid of in hopes that it will desensitize them through repeated exposure. Over time, what was once seen as somewhat frightening will begin to feel much more normal and manageable, and in the process the fears that once ruled us will begin to fade into the background.

Immersion therapy exercises are designed to push us outside of our comfort zones where we feel safe, protected, and unthreatened. We all have various comfort zones in our personal and professional lives that keep us insulated from our fears. By confronting the things that frighten us the most, however, we are learning to push ourselves to leave those comfort zones behind, bringing a bit of self-induced adversity and challenge to our lives.

While operating inside our comfort zones we can still manage to accomplish a lot in life. This is the setting within which we feel most at ease and self-assured, operating with confidence and control. But many of the tasks that we take on that fall within that zone can be completed with little thought or effort. They don't tend to test us in any way, nor do they force us to grow personally or professionally. And while we may be able to achieve great things while remaining safely ensconced in our comfort zone, chances are we won't live up to our full potential while we remain there either.

Stepping outside of your comfort zone almost always comes with risks. That alone can be a scary proposition, as it brings uncertainty and forces us to step into the unknown. Things that were once predictable and easy become more difficult and challenging, and we're no longer able to just coast along on the talents and skills we already possess. Instead, we have to expand our capabilities, learn new things, and embrace the fears that have held us back.

By giving up the safety of our comfort zone we're also willingly giving up the control and predictability that we've come to know and trust in favor of potentially bigger and more satisfying rewards. In order to do that, we have to learn to accept that we may have to face some of our biggest fears as part of that process. When embarking along a new path, success is far from assured and what the future holds will always remain a mystery. But, in doing so we are also shaking ourselves free from the shackles of a safe existence for the chance to achieve bigger and better things.

66

I'm not afraid of storms,
for I'm learning to sail
my ship."

—Louisa May Alcott

The challenges that fall outside our personal comfort zones will be quite different for each and every one of us. Something that is mundane and simple for one person, may be completely terrifying and exhilarating for someone else. A race car driver, for example, may find that driving along at 200 miles per hour on a track is a completely normal thing to do. But ask him or her to get up in front of a class and teach basic driving skills to strangers, and that same person may turn into a bundle of nerves.

Familiarity creates a feeling of ease and comfort, while doing things that we're not accustomed to can often rattle even the most confident person. But that's what getting outside your comfort zone is all about. It's a chance to explore your own personal boundaries and find ways to push beyond them, which is where we find the most opportunity to grow and change.

Perhaps you're thinking of starting a new business, training to run a marathon, or learning a foreign language. No matter where your motivations are found, the fears that come along with embarking on this new path are often the same. We wonder if we are smart enough, talented enough, or dedicated enough to see our goals through to the end. We weigh our chances for success closely before we take the leap, all the while hoping that we'll land on our feet. We are in fact embracing our fear of the unknown with the hopes of it paying off by accomplishing our goals.

One of the first things that any Navy SEAL candidate learns when he begins Basic Underwater Demolitions/SEAL (BUD/S) training is to get comfortable being uncomfortable. In other words, they have to learn to abandon their comfort zones and embrace their fears if they want to survive BUD/S and eventually pin the coveted SEAL trident onto their uniform. For trainees, being uncomfortable quickly becomes the new norm and if they can't find a way to adapt, they'll exit the program in short order. But those who can learn to push themselves harder will soon discover that they can achieve things they probably didn't even know they were capable of before they started.

This is a philosophy that will stick with a SEAL for his entire career, spurring him to leave his comfort zone on a regular basis in effort to evolve and grow as a warrior. A SEAL can't afford to become complacent or content with his skills and training but must always look for new challenges and opportunities to improve instead. By accepting that being uncomfortable is simply a way of life, he learns to widen his personal comfort zone into new areas, while also expanding the things that he is capable of along the way.

Most people do not have a profession that by its very nature pushes them to get outside of their comfort zone on a regular basis. Instead, they have to choose to do so themselves from time to time. The hope is that by doing so we'll improve as individuals and learn to embrace the things that frighten us the most. In order to do that we must summon up as much courage and confidence as we can, and be willing to take a chance on ourselves, even when the outcome is uncertain and far from assured.

The rewards for leaving your comfort zone behind are many. Venturing outside of your safe harbor can bring a sense of excitement and renewed enthusiasm as you look to embrace the challenge of the unknown. And when you learn to function in this strange new space, you'll also grow in confidence and strength. You'll be reminded that shaking things up from time to time can be good for you both professionally and personally, giving you the chance to grow while gaining a better understanding of your own capabilities and limitations. That alone can make the entire experience an enriching one.

Make no mistake, stepping outside of your comfort zone will be incredibly unsettling at times. You may find yourself feeling vulnerable, overwhelmed, and ready to retreat back to the safety and predictability of your normal life. But if you pause to take a deep breath, remind yourself that you can control your fears, and focus on your goals, you'll likely discover that things may not be quite as terrifying as you once thought.

In our daily lives, the comfort zones that we've built for ourselves serve as a shield against some of our most common fears. While operating within those zones we are well protected from our fear of failure, our fear of the unknown, and our fear of change. Each of those fears can be a significant roadblock to our success, preventing us from pursuing our objectives fully. As long as we are content to stay rooted in our safe bubble, we can't truly face them or learn to overcome them. In which case, those fears will continue to hold sway over us.

The process of embracing those fundamental fears starts with accepting the fact that when we leave our comfort zones behind, we are probably going to fail from time to time. We won't always be able to predict what is going to happen, and it is important to understand that our lives could change in some significant ways. But along the way we'll also be learning from our mistakes, gaining valuable insights into who we are, and pushing ourselves in new and exciting ways.

One of the other benefits of getting comfortable with being uncomfortable is that you'll discover that your once small and confining comfort zone will suddenly start to naturally expand in size. Things that routinely made you feel anxious and afraid in the past will no longer be quite so intimidating or frightening. You'll become accustomed to embracing your fears and testing your limits to the point that it will no longer feel quite so unnatural to tackle the unknown. Instead, you may find that there is an enormous sense of self satisfaction that comes from personal growth and achieving the things that you've set your mind too.

"

Do one thing every day
that scares you."

—Eleanor Roosevelt

Just about anyone can benefit from learning to embrace their fears and leave their comfort zone behind on a regular basis, including individuals who have already set high marks in terms of achievement. Take for example professional rock climber Alex Honnold, who is widely seen as one of the most talented and accomplished climbers of his generation. Over the course of his career, Alex has made incredible ascents on some of the most difficult routes in the world, occasionally setting speed records along the way. But in June of 2017, he did something that no one else has ever done before, redefining what it truly means to leave safety and comfort behind.

Born in Sacramento, California, Honnold started his climbing career at the tender age of five when he took up the sport at a local gym. As a child, he was a good climber, but Honnold himself has said that many of his peers were stronger and more naturally gifted. Still, he stuck with the sport and continued to hone his skills into his teenage years.

After graduating from high school in 2003, Honnold went off to the University of California at Berkley where he enrolled as an engineering student.

But in his first year of college the young freshman was hit with a double dose of hardship. First, his maternal grandfather passed away and then soon thereafter his parents announced that they were getting divorced. As you can imagine, this was a very difficult time for Alex, who often found solace by skipping class to go climbing by himself.

After a year at Berkley, Honnold quit school and decided to travel around California to go rock climbing instead. He often found himself camping in Yosemite National Park, which is home to some of the biggest and most iconic climbing routes in the entire world. The rock faces on El Capitan and Half Dome lure some of the best climbers from around the globe on an annual basis, and Alex soon found himself amongst them.

Over time, Honnold's prowess as a climber grew and began to garner him quite a bit of attention. Within the climbing community he earned himself a reputation for not only being fast and precise but daring as well. Soon, he was recognized as one of the best free soloists in the world, which is the most difficult and dangerous climbing style of them all.

Despite that, however, Alex always came across as very humble, generally downplaying his extraordinary accomplishments.

Most of the top rock climbers in the world are free climbers. That means that they make their ascents using ropes, harnesses, and other safety equipment, but that gear is there just to ensure that they don't fall. Free soloists, on the other hand, don't use any gear at all, including ropes. They simply climb using nothing more than their hands and feet, relying solely on their own skills to help them reach the top. This type of climbing requires laser focus and a very high degree of concentration and mental toughness, because just one slip can prove to be disastrous.

Some of Alex's biggest and boldest climbs have been done while free soloing. For instance, in 2007 he climbed a 1,200-foot wall in Zion National Park without using a rope and followed that up a few months later with a free solo ascent of a 2,000-foot wall on Yosemite's Half Dome. At that point, even other top climbers were starting to take note of Honnold's accomplishments as his level of respect within the community continued to grow.

You would think that a climber who takes on some of the toughest routes in the world without using a rope would probably have a very wide comfort zone. After all, Honnold routinely finds himself hundreds of feet off the ground with only his own considerable talents and skills preventing him from plummeting to his death. But even someone who possesses such a high level of ability, not to mention nerves of steel, still looks for new challenges from time to time. In this case, that means finding even bigger and more difficult routes to climb.

For Honnold, that big challenge came in June of 2017 when he completed the first ever free solo ascent of El Capitan in Yosemite. Alex made this groundbreaking climb along a 3,000-foot route known as Free Rider, which typically takes most rock climbers three to five days to complete. Alex did it in three hours and fifty-six minute.

What made this such an awe-inspiring climb wasn't how fast he went up the route, however. Instead, it was the fact that Honnold was able to scale what is arguably the most iconic climbing wall in the world without using ropes, a harness, or any other gear. He simply climbed in shorts, a t-shirt, and climbing shoes, with a chalk bag attached to his belt to help keep his hands dry. No one had ever tried to free solo such a big route before, as the mere thought of being thousands of feet off the ground, without any kind of safety equipment to arrest his fall, seemed like a ludicrous proposition.

Make no mistake, climbing Free Rider was a push outside of Alex's comfort zone. Yes, he had free soloed other big routes in the past, but nothing that was as long and difficult as an ascent of El Capitan. No one was sure if such a feat were even possible and the consequences for failure could have been catastrophic. One wrong move—one lapse in concentration—would have ended in tragedy. Yet Honnold was able to maintain his composure and his mental toughness all the way to the top, finishing what fellow climber Tommy Caldwell called the "moon landing" of free soloing and writer Daniel Duane of the *New York Times* described as "One of the great athletic feats of any kind, ever."

Honnold's big leap outside his comfort zone didn't come without plenty of thought and planning. The climber himself would tell you that it was a well-calculated risk, as he had practiced on

Free Rider countless times, learning every move and memorizing the hand and footholds he'd use on his way to the top. In this way, he was as prepared as he could possibly be, although he still had to actually make the climb without ropes for it to actually count. He has also said that he was nervous before he started the climb and got tense on some of the more challenging sections. Those are telltale signs of someone who is most definitely outside his comfort zone.

"

The shell must break before the bird can fly."

—Alfred Tennyson

Despite being one of the best climbers in the world, and having free soloed big walls before, failure was still a possibility. Honnold had actually attempted the same climb a few months earlier and abandoned the attempt when the conditions didn't feel right. Instead, he chose to rope up and get back down safely, rather than push through when things weren't necessarily going his way.

There are a couple of lessons to be learned there when it comes to us stepping outside of our comfort zones. First, Honnold failed on his first serious attempt, but was able to come back later and still reach his goal. We need to remind ourselves of that when we come up short in the pursuit of our objectives. Just because we failed the first time, that doesn't mean we will again in the future.

The other takeaway from Alex's first attempt at Free Rider is that he knew when to throw in the towel and call it a day. He knew that it was best to play it safe and get off the wall in one piece rather than press his luck when things weren't feeling right. This allowed him to return later with renewed confidence and enthusiasm. The next time he gave it a go, he was healthier, better prepared, and ready to make history.

Keep that in mind when you're operating outside your comfort zone as well. If things aren't feeling right, it is okay to trust your instincts, back off, and regroup. This will give you the opportunity to tackle your goals at another time, perhaps coming at them with a new plan of attack and a better sense of how to succeed.

After his free solo of El Capitan, Honnold admitted that physically speaking the climb itself wasn't particularly tough. He is well conditioned for those types of challenges and has spent many hours on rock walls before. It was incredibly demanding mentally, however, forcing him to focus intently for nearly four hours, knowing full well that he had to get everything just right. But in preparing to make the ascent he became laser focused on achieving his goal, which gave him an incredibly tough mindset. In a way, while preparing for the climb he wasn't just working out his body, but his mind too. And just like the muscles in his arms, legs, and chest, his brain grew stronger as well.

That is one of the benefits of facing your fears. Because you are pushing yourself to try new things, achieve big goals, and leave your comfort zone behind, you're also learning to be more mentally focused and agile. You'll gain confidence and learn a lot about yourself along the way too, making it easier to take on the things that scare you the most in future endeavors.

They say that familiarity breeds contempt and by taking the steps to embrace your fears you're also learning how to understand them better. As you get more familiar with the things that frighten you, you're also likely to want to break free of those fears all the more. Often we come to realize that many of our fears are rooted in our lack of self-confidence. We're afraid of failure because we don't think we're good enough to achieve the things we want. We're afraid of the unknown because we don't trust ourselves to be able to navigate our way past challenges that we didn't anticipate. And we're afraid of change because we think that we're not smart or gifted or experienced enough to adapt to new challenges.

By embracing our fears we're not only learning

to put them behind us, but we're also putting a little faith in ourselves and our own abilities. When you begin to believe in yourself, the fears that hold us in place become less of an obstacle.

PART III

LETTING GO OF FEAR

Embracing our fears gives us the ability to become intimately familiar with them, while learning a lot more about ourselves in the process. By examining the roots of those fears, we can start to understand them better, which is useful when we're trying to find ways to release the hold that they have on us. This can help us to overcome our fright to a degree, and press forward towards our goals, which are often put on hold because the things we are afraid of paralyze us into inaction.

But embracing our fears isn't the same as learning to let go of them. Even as we summon the courage we need to chase our goals, we're still allowing those fears to linger inside of us. This allows them to maintain some level of control over us even after we've found ways to manage that fear. To truly lead a fearless life, we have to eventually learn to let go of the phobias that have a negative impact on us, freeing us up to accomplish everything we want to do.

Most of the fears that create obstacles in our life are grounded in a lack of confidence, an overabundance of uncertainty, and doubt. The voice inside our head tells us we're not good enough, talented enough, or smart enough to be successful, so we just accept our place in life and don't try to strive for anything more. The reality is, all of us have the ability to lead richer, more fulfilling lives if we just learn to tune those voices out and have a little faith in ourselves.

Building confidence is an important key to overcoming the crippling self-doubt that many of us struggle with. That confidence begins with the process of learning to face our fears and take a leap outside of our comfort zones from time to time. In doing so, we start to see that we're capable of so much more than we first imagined, which allows us to set the bar even higher and go after even bigger goals. Eventually the process becomes a familiar one as you conquer one challenge and start looking for the next.

The use of micro-goals to achieve macro-goals is something that has guided my life and allowed me to accomplish more than I ever would have otherwise. Essentially, this means setting a monumental goal for yourself and then outlining all of the smaller steps you need to achieve in order to make that goal a reality. Those smaller steps are the micro-goals that serve as the building blocks to success. And because they are bite-sized objectives, they don't seem quite as daunting to accomplish.

"

Courage is resistance to fear, mastery of fear, not absence of fear."

—Mark Twain

An example of this process is setting a goal to run a marathon. In the beginning, you may not be able to run more than a mile or two without stopping. Your first goal is to learn to pace yourself so you can cover those distances without needing a break. Once you do that, you can ramp up to three miles or try to finish the same distance in a faster time. Eventually, your body will adapt to the exercise and begin to get into better condition, making a one or two-mile run seem easy. That's when you set the next micro-goal of increasing your distance to three, four, five, or even more miles. Over time you'll be able to use this process to build up to 26.2 miles, the distance of a full marathon.

By accomplishing your micro-goals you're also earning a series of micro-successes. This has the added benefit of slowly, but steadily, building your confidence level, which can provide the extra dose of courage you need to go after increasingly larger goals. Once you have proven to yourself that you can indeed do the things you set your mind to, it makes it much easier to continue to pursue your objectives. Over time, those small boosts of confidence can really start to add up, improving your self-esteem and building trust in your own strengths and abilities.

In the case of the beginner runner, that means that once he or she demonstrates to themselves that they can run a mile or two without having to stop, it becomes easier to ratchet their goals even higher. They've learned that they can push themselves to continue running, even when they are uncomfortable and their body is telling them to stop. That ability automatically scales up as the mileage increases, allowing them to run longer distances in a shorter time.

For a Navy SEAL, the process of using microsuccesses to build confidence starts in Basic Underwater Demolitions/SEAL training. At the beginning of the six-month-long program most of the candidates already have some degree of trepidation, as the level of difficulty for BUD/S is well known ahead of time. Many of the trainees will question whether or not they have what it takes to get through the training, which puts a high emphasis on both physical and mental challenges.

The dropout rate for BUD/S is extremely high, with only about 20 percent of the class making it through to graduation on average. Those that do survive the training often do so not because they are the strongest or most gifted athletes but are instead the most mentally tough. That starts with having the confidence in themselves to push through, even when they are feeling uncomfortable and uncertain. The more often they are able to do that, and successfully complete a training evolution, the more they come to trust in their own abilities.

Due to the constant training and honing of their skills, SEALs tend to be very confident individuals. That confidence comes from being pushed to their limits, both physically and mentally, on a regular basis. By being as prepared as humanly possible, and routinely facing extremely demanding situations, they learn to let go of their fears and trust in their training and skills. On a mission, there is very little room for fear or doubt, which is why these men learn to let those emotions go and focus on accomplishing their objectives instead.

Increasing your level of confidence comes with experience and time. By stepping outside of your comfort zone on a regular basis, you'll start to get the experience you need and by achieving your objectives you'll start to trust your instincts and abilities more fully. When that starts to happen, your confidence levels grow accordingly.

It is then that your fears will start to take a backseat, and even though they remain a part of you, they begin to loom less large. They may still have some sway over your decision-making process, but they no longer hold you back as they once did. Because you have proven to yourself that you can overcome your doubts, those fears are no longer an anchor that is holding you in place. They may still act as brakes, slowing you down and impeding progress on occasion, but they don't offer the same level of paralysis as in the past.

By establishing a track record for success, we become more confident not just in our decision-making process, but also our ability to achieve our objectives. We also learn to trust our ability to accurately assess our own abilities, discovering that is an incredibly useful tool to have at our disposal.

Two important tools that every Navy SEAL possesses are a strong mindset and the ability to accurately assess their own skills and talents. In a lot of ways, these two abilities go hand-in-hand, giving a SEAL an unusually high level of awareness when it comes to his strengths and weaknesses. It also allows him to understand his limitations, which is crucial for knowing how far he can push himself both in training and while on a mission.

As already discussed, the ability to self-assess also helps a SEAL to recognize the deficiencies in his knowledge and training and look for ways to overcome those gaps. In doing so, he's learning to put his own fears and uncertainty aside as he improves both professionally and personally. To be the best at his job, a SEAL knows that there are always things that he can improve on and with the knowledge he quietly gains confidence in his capabilities to succeed where others might fail.

A powerful mindset brings a high level of self-discipline as well. It gives a SEAL the ability to face fear and uncertainty, yet still control his emotions and focus on the objectives that he has been tasked with. Invariably, at some point during his training, nearly every SEAL candidate will hear an inner voice telling him that he isn't good enough or strong enough to make it through an exercise. Those who have the mental discipline to control those voices and silence the doubts are able to continue on. Those who can't, will almost certainly wash out.

When venturing outside our comfort zone, those same voices tend to pop up in our heads as well. They are the voices that force us to question our abilities and lose confidence in ourselves. Learning how to manage that inner dialogue is a crucial part of having the courage to press on with our plans and begin to permanently let go of our fears. That starts with having confidence, discipline, and a strong mindset, all of which can substantially alter the narrative that we create for ourselves.

One of the things that SEAL candidates learn at an early stage is to turn their inner dialog into a positive one. Too often, the thoughts that pervade our minds are negative in nature, hence the reason people tend to generate so much self-doubt. But by learning to control the conversation, and in positive, reassuring tones, you can begin the process of strengthening your mind and shift the conversation away from an *I can't do this* attitude towards an *I will do this* mindset.

This same approach can help us in achieving our goals too. The power of positive thinking can go a long way towards instilling the self-confidence we need to not only achieve our goals, but to permanently let go of our fears too. Negative thoughts bring anxiety and doubt, but a positive inner dialog can be encouraging, calming, and provide the strength we need to reassure ourselves we're heading in the right direction. The more positive reinforcement that we give ourselves, the more we'll start to believe in our own abilities. Soon, success starts to become a self-fulfilling prophecy, with our fears fading out as a result.

"

He who has overcome his fears will truly be free."

—Aristotle

A famous example of how developing a positive mindset can help you succeed in life comes from actor and comedian Jim Carrey. In 1990, Carrey was still new to Hollywood and was struggling to make a name for himself. At night, he would often drive up into the hills surrounding Los Angeles and look down at the city below, dreaming about becoming a star. He was broke, had few prospects, and was still looking for his first big break. But he was also optimistic, willing to work hard, and had set enormous objectives for himself.

On one of his trips up into the Hollywood Hills, Carrey began thinking about those goals and his future in showbiz. Up until that point, he hadn't had much success finding suitable roles and it would have been easy for him to let the negative voices inside his head create doubt about his future. Instead, he took out his checkbook and wrote a check to himself for ten million dollars, dating it for November 1995, exactly five years into the future. It was a positive message to himself about his confidence in his own talents and his ability to succeed.

The comedian took that check, which was written for "acting services rendered," and put it in his wallet. From time to time over the next few years, he'd come across it there and it served as inspiration for him to keep working towards his goals. As the years passed, the check became a little dog-eared and faded, but it remained a constant reminder that he still had work to do when it came to achieving his objectives for his career.

Late in 1990 Carrey became a regular cast member of the ensemble sketch show *In Living Color*, and during its four-year run he grew into one of its breakout stars. During that time, Carrey would create some of the show's most memorable characters, striking a chord with the audience. This eventually led to him starring in several comedy movies that were released in 1994, including *Ace Ventura: Pet Detective* and *The Mask*. Both films were hits with movie goers, making the comedian a rising star in the process.

Carrey's next project was a film called *Dumb and Dumber*, which would cement him as one of the most bankable comedic actors in Hollywood. When he signed on to make the film, he learned that his payday would be ten million dollars, by far his biggest to date. He earned that role in November

1995, five years after he had written himself that check, which he still carried with him in his wallet.

Obviously, Carrey has proven himself to be a comedic talent and a gifted actor. His films have earned hundreds of millions of dollars at the box-office and made him an international star. Early in his career, however, it felt like those goals were completely out of reach, which would have caused many people to abandon their dreams. Carrey didn't lose focus on his goals, however, and used a positive mindset to help achieve them. By writing that ten million dollar check he was in a sense betting on himself and his future. Ultimately that paid off for him in spectacular fashion, turning him into one of the biggest movie stars on the planet.

No doubt there were times when Carrey experienced a real fear of failing. At no point did it seem that success was assured, even as his profile as an actor and comedian continued to grow. He used a positive mindset, combined with a strong work ethic, to overcome those fears. He knew that in order to achieve the things he wanted in life, he couldn't let anything hold him back, least of all lingering doubt and fear over his own abilities.

In addition to using a positive mindset and controlling his own inner dialogue, Carrey used another technique that is commonly employed by Navy SEALs. We've already mentioned the power of visualization as a tool to help us explore various challenges and anticipate roadblocks that may come our way, but that same technique can be used to help reinforce positive thinking as well. In this case, Carrey was able to visualize his future success long before he started his movie career. This helped to give him the confidence that he needed to continue on even when things weren't going his way.

Of course, he was also able to accurately assess his own strengths and weaknesses as well, which allowed him to hone his acting and comedic chops. While Carrey had confidence in his abilities, he knew that he had to work on his skills as an actor and his comedic timing too. To do that, he took acting classes and worked out his stand-up act on stage in local comedy clubs, becoming a much better entertainer as a result.

In other words, he didn't just write himself that famous ten-million-dollar check and expect the universe would bring success to his doorstep. Instead, he harnessed the power of positive thinking, was self-disciplined enough to know he had to work hard and took the necessary steps to acquire the skills and abilities he needed. It wasn't enough to just want to succeed, he had to proactively go out and earn it too. That meant learning to let go of his fears and take bold steps towards his eventual success.

"

Do the thing you fear to do and keep on doing it. That is the quickest and surest way ever discovered to conquer fear."

—Dale Carnegie

Letting go of your fears isn't an easy thing to do, even when you have a clear vision of what you want to accomplish. It requires a tough mindset, a positive outlook, and the ability to persevere even when it seems like the deck is stacked against you. If you can develop those capabilities within yourself, you'll definitely be on the path to achieving your objectives, which is exactly what Navy SEALs do as part of their training.

The SEAL candidates that learn to adopt those traits as quickly as possible have a much better chance of successfully completing BUD/S. By design, the program is incredibly demanding throughout, which is why there is such a high attrition rate. But things get especially difficult in week three of training, because that's when Hell Week begins. Over the course of the following five and a half days, the candidates face almost nonstop activity, including running, swimming, paddling, hauling boats up and down the beach, doing push-ups, sit-ups, pull-ups, rope climbs, obstacle course runs and other physically demanding exercises. It is without a doubt one of the most difficult obstacles that prospective SEALs face, with many struggling to complete the exercise.

During Hell Week, a BUD/S class will spend roughly 20–22 hours a day training, with the SEAL candidates running as many as 200 miles over the course of that five-day period. The members of the class are cold, wet, and tired most of that entire time, which is why so many of them don't make it past that point of their training. Those who are ready to call it quits must go to the center of the training courtyard, place their helmet on the ground, and ring a large bell three times, that is prominently displayed there. In doing so, they signal that they have had enough and are ready to exit the program altogether.

Those who manage to survive Hell Week do so because they are able to not just endure the physical challenges but more importantly the mental ones too. They have a tough enough mindset to help them ignore the pain and discomfort, and press on with their training, even when their body is screaming for them to quit. They also have the ability to accurately assess their own abilities and know when they can safely push themselves harder or need to back off and give themselves time to recuperate. Maintaining a positive outlook on their prospects certainly helps too and plays a significant role in their ability to visualize themselves making it through the grueling week in one piece.

Hell Week is so tough on the body and mind that by the time it is over half of the candidates who started the BUD/S class have already elected to ring out. Those who remain face another four weeks of the toughest training imaginable as Phase 1 endlessly drags on. During that time, they will continue to work on their physical conditioning, mental strength, teamwork, and competency in the water. Four-mile timed runs on a soft-sand beach, two-mile timed swims in the cold ocean, and a challenging obstacle course are used to measure a candidate's progress and overall aptitude. The stronger and more disciplined they become, the more their confidence grows.

By the time Hell Week is over, a fraction of the men who started BUD/S training remain. Those who move on to Phase 2 of the program spend the next seven weeks learning the intricacies and art of combat diving. That's followed up with another seven-week course that focuses on land warfare, with a focus on hand-to-hand combat, maritime demolitions, and small-arms tactics. Of course the physical and mental training continues to become more challenging too as the men take their next steps towards earning their coveted SEAL trident.

Following Phase 1, the BUD/S dropout rate drops off substantially. Some candidates will continue to ring the bell during the subsequent phases, but most of the individuals who make it through the first seven weeks are better prepared for what comes after. At that point, their confidence levels rise significantly and their belief in their own abilities continue to grow as well. They know that they've made it through what is known as the toughest military training in the world and as a result, their doubts begin to fade. By then, they've also moved considerably beyond their previous comfort zones as well, taking a massive step towards conquering their biggest fears along the way.

Being a Navy SEAL is a high-stakes, high-stress profession that requires discipline, focus, and quick thinking. Fear can short circuit those traits, causing individuals to panic and lose control at crucial moments. Those reactions are simply unacceptable during an operation, which is why SEALs train their minds to be often times stronger than their bodies. In doing so, they learn to control, channel, and eventually let go of their fears, which allows them to stay calm and maintain their composure even during very chaotic and otherwise frightening circumstances.

Professional athletes often talk about how they can reach a certain point in their career where it feels like the game is starting to slow down around them. In actuality, the action on the field is moving just as fast as it always has, but over time the player's brain adapts to that pace, allowing them to see and process more in a split second than they could when they were first starting out. That is due to the level of discipline, confidence, and focus that comes along with experience and continued training and preparation. This in turn gives them the ability to remain calm and poised even in stressful situations.

A similar thing happens to SEALs as they continue to train and gain experience, too. Their ability to process what is happening around them in a clear, concise, and accurate manner helps them to become extremely proficient at their jobs. In stressful situations—such as a firefight or a hostage rescue—it can often feel like time is slowing down for them as well. This makes it easier to assess what is happening and react appropriately without hesitation or doubt.

For athletes and Navy SEALs, this perceived slowing of time is a result of learning to channel their fears and remain calm amidst the chaos that is happening around them. By facing similar situations during training, they become familiar with what to expect, which helps to remove some of the uncertainty and doubt. Even while they are in the heat of the moment there is no sense of panic, just a calm, professional demeanor that can see them through even the most frenetic of experiences.

This is the mindset that allows a quarterback to recognize which opposing player is coming at him on a blitz and learn to compensate for that attack. Meanwhile, he can simultaneously read the defensive coverage to find the best match-up for his wide receivers, signaling to them which routes to take down the field. This all occurs in just a few seconds, so when the ball is snapped, and there is controlled chaos all around him, he can still calmly survey the entire field before making a decision on what to do.

Similarly, a SEAL has the same uncanny ability to survey a battlefield, recognize active threats, and identify points of tactical importance all in the blink of an eye. Thanks to his training, that same SEAL can identify a proper course of action, while also considering potential contingencies based on enemy reactions and potential changes to these conditions. Much like a quarterback, he learns to convey his assessment to his teammates, allowing them to efficiently work in conjunction with one another in an effort to complete the mission.

This uncanny ability to avoid getting rattled during stressful—and often hectic—situations is a direct result of having a tough "combat" mindset, a high degree of confidence, experience, and training. These are traits that SEALs and top athletes share with one another, although those individuals certainly don't have a monopoly on that skillset. Quite the contrary, in fact, as we can all learn to incorporate these same traits into our lives and use them to master the fears that could be holding us back.

66

Fear isn't an excuse to
come to a standstill. It is
the impetus to step up
and strike."

—Arthur Ashe

As you learn to get comfortable being uncomfortable, you will also start to experience your own version of time slowing down around you. The longer and more regularly we operate outside of our personal comfort zones, the more adept we'll get at thinking on our feet, learning to react quickly to challenges, and finding ways to function even while under duress. Over time, this typically leads to a significant gain in confidence as our faith in ourselves and our ability to adapt to changing situations grows. It is also an important step towards permanently letting go of our fears as we face down the things that once frightened us the most.

Those increasing levels of confidence play a big role in demystifying the hold that our fears have over us. Once we begin to turn our goals into successes, we also discover that the fears that once held us back aren't quite as insurmountable as we once thought. The fear of failure is less daunting as your belief in your abilities increases, making it seem less risky when you embark on a new challenge.

Tackling our fear of uncertainty and change starts with improving our self-confidence as well. Not knowing what the future holds will always be a little unsettling, but once you've had some experience dealing with the unexpected obstacles that crop up, it becomes increasingly easier to take those challenges in stride. If you can clear those hurdles and still continue moving forward, the level of self-assurance you'll have when launching a new project will be much higher. You won't necessarily be any better at anticipating the changes that could be coming your way, but you will feel more comfortable tackling them head on as they arise.

Beyond just growing our self-confidence and gaining experience, some of the other techniques we've already outlined—most notably visualization and maintaining a positive mindset—can help eliminate fear as well. By imagining potential future outcomes—both good and bad—we can mentally prepare ourselves for the things we might face down the line. This allows us to create a sense of familiarity that make it far less terrifying to leave our comfort zone behind and strike out for unfamiliar territory.

It is nearly impossible to overstate the importance of maintaining a positive mindset when it comes to dealing with fear. Much of the doubt and uncertainty that we feel is directly related to the fact that our brains naturally gravitate toward negative and discouraging thoughts. More often than not we are our own worst critics, creating our own obstacles to success and generating unfounded fears in our own minds. But maintaining a positive outlook can dramatically change that by not just pushing past the negativity, but also reinforcing the idea that we are talented and hardworking individuals who will find a way to succeed.

The power of positive thinking is drilled into a SEAL's mindset early on, reminding him that he is capable of achieving great things. Negative thoughts are counterproductive, serving only to bring him and the team down. But by remaining calm, staying positive, and reminding himself that he possesses unique skill and abilities, it is possible for a SEAL to get through some of the most difficult circumstances imaginable without giving in to negative thoughts that could create doubt.

Both negative and positive thoughts have a way of turning into self-fulfilling prophecies. If you think you're going to fail, there is a good chance you will. On the other hand, if you remain upbeat, keep an open mind, and stay positive, there is a much better chance that you'll achieve the things that you set your mind to. Adopting that kind of approach will help vanquish your doubts, freeing you up to focus on other things.

Part of having a tough mental attitude is finding ways to stay positive even while facing overwhelming odds. A SEAL's ability to control his own inner dialogue plays an important role here as well, allowing him to reinforce positive thoughts and ignore fears and doubts. The trick is to realize you don't have to eliminate the voices you hear, but instead turn them from a negative force into a reassuring one. While most of us hear our inner thoughts telling us we aren't good enough or we don't deserve success, a SEAL tells himself that he's got what it takes to reach his goals and that everything is going to be alright, even during extremely stressful circumstances.

For a SEAL, this ability is reinforced during a particularly notorious training session called the pool competency test, or "pool comp." This challenge takes place during Phase 2, Dive Phase, and involves SEAL instructors pouncing on a candidate while in the pool. Those instructors disorient the trainee by holding him down under water, putting him in a tight choke-hold, pulling off his dive mask, tearing off his fins and weight belt and then pulling the regulator out of his mouth and tying the breathing hose into a knot.

Since he is underwater, the trainee has only a limited amount of time to act and rectify the situation. He must clear his mind, stay calm, and remind himself that everything is going to be okay. Then, he'll get to work on untying the knot and restoring his breathing apparatus before he runs out of air. If he returns to the surface before accomplishing that task, he fails the training exercise.

The pool comp test plays on a deep-seated fear of drowning that nearly all of us share. The idea of running out of air while submerged underwater is enough to cause panic and confusion in just about anyone. A Navy SEAL doesn't have the luxury of losing control, however, particularly when conducting an important operation. The test reinforces the importance of staying focused and maintaining a positive mindset. Negativity will only serve to slow him down at a time when every second counts and succumbing to fear could be tantamount to disaster.

Most SEAL trainees fail the pool comp test on their first attempt, even though they may have some idea of when it is coming. Fortunately for them they are given a second chance at it, with the resilient ones learning from the mistakes they may have made the first time around. Having been through the experience once before helps to take some of the fear of the unknown out of the equation and proves once again that experience can help us overcome challenges. Those who do find success during pool comp usually do so because they have mastered the ability to remain positive and clear headed even when things aren't necessarily going as planned.

"

A pessimist sees difficulty in every opportunity, an optimist sees the opportunity in every difficulty."

—Winston Churchill

Using your inner dialogue to create a more positive outlook isn't a technique that only SEALs can benefit from. In fact, just about all of us can use this skill to help us reach our goals and vanquish our fears. Adopting a positive mindset is a powerful tool that can have a deep and lasting impact on all aspects of our lives.

Those with a pessimistic approach tend to internalize their setbacks, placing the blame on themselves when things don't go their way. The voices in their head tell them that they aren't talented enough or haven't worked hard enough to reach their goals. This can be incredibly discouraging, forcing us to retreat back into our comfort zones, possibly never to come out again.

In contrast to that, someone with a positive disposition tends to take a more open-minded approach when things don't go their way. They can assess their performance more accurately and understand that even when they do everything correctly things still might not work out in their favor. That doesn't mean that they choose to give up completely, however. It simply means that they have to try again, this time working a little harder and building on what they've learned.

So how exactly does staying positive help you to begin to let go of your fears? When you have a "can-do" attitude and feel that setbacks are only temporary obstacles to be overcome, it is much easier to let go of the things we are afraid of. Failure and uncertainty aren't quite so unsettling when your mind has learned to accept them. Instead of being permanent impediments to your goals, those roadblocks are viewed as learning experiences and opportunities to test your knowledge and skills. In the end, they make you stronger and better equipped to deal with adversity.

Our growing confidence and experience can make us feel like we can accomplish just about anything, which can be incredibly empowering. The flip side of that is that it can also introduce another fear that we may not have anticipated—the fear of having a dependence on others.

Many of us are afraid to ask for help as we think it might make us look weak, indecisive, or untalented. The reality is, the opposite is actually true. Knowing when to seek the advice and assistance of others is a sign of wisdom, once again demonstrating how important it is to be able to assess our own strengths and weaknesses. Recognizing that someone else has the skills and knowledge that we need, and then tapping them for assistance simply means we are working smarter and becoming more resourceful.

Throughout his BUD/S training, a SEAL is taught many of the skills he needs to be a formidable warrior on the battlefield. His physical training is amongst the very best in the world and he is shown multiple techniques designed to build a mentally tough mindset. This alone is enough to make him an independent and resourceful person who is able to achieve great things without assistance from anyone else.

That said, no SEAL can ever reach his full potential until he learns to properly operate within a team. Teamwork is a major part of what makes the SEALs such a force to contend with on the battlefield. Each man knows his role and the entire unit works in conjunction with one another to achieve the objective they've been assigned. There is no room for ego or bravado, and no one is afraid to ask for help or seek out the assistance of one of his team-mates. That's because each of them knows that two SEALs working together aren't just twice as efficient as they are on their own but are instead orders of magnitude better. And when you put a whole team of SEALs together, there is very little that they can't accomplish.

"

Fear has two meanings:
'Forget everything and
run' or 'Face everything
and rise.' The choice is
yours."

—Zig Ziglar

When it comes to striving towards our own goals, we need to learn to put aside our fear of asking for help and learn to admit when the assistance of others is needed. In doing so, we can take goals that previously seemed out of reach and make them much more accessible. Additionally, when moving outside of our comfort zones, it is always easier to do so with someone else at our side rather than having to totally go it alone. Facing your fears and learning to let go of them isn't quite so intimidating if you have someone supporting your efforts.

Using teamwork to achieve our objectives can take many different forms. If you've set a goal to run a marathon, joining a running group or asking a friend to serve as a training partner can prove incredibly useful. Those types of arrangements end up providing some much-needed accountability and companionship, which can make the experience a more rewarding one for everyone involved.

A runner may even consider hiring a coach to help correct their stride or create a personal workout schedule to help them to be better prepared. While technically you can learn to do most of those things completely on your own, it is far more efficient and wise to seek out the assistance of someone who already has the knowledge and experience we're looking for.

When starting a business it is always good to have partners or staff that can help guide you through the precarious early days of such an endeavor. If you're looking to become more fit or lose weight, consulting with a dietitian or personal trainer can provide amazing insights into how you should proceed. If your goal is to become a professional photographer, you might sign up for a photography class at your local community college or consult with someone who is already working in the field. The point is, most of us rarely possess all of the skills and knowledge we need to achieve everything we want in life, so we need to be able ask for help from time to time.

Admitting that we need assistance isn't easy, but it can be incredibly beneficial, as the advice and insights we receive can make all of the difference when it comes to making progress towards our goals. The idea that two heads are better than one is never more evident than when you're looking for creative ways to overcome an obstacle. When that happens, having a knowledgeable partner to bounce ideas off of can be invaluable.

As with all things, the experience we gain when we learn from others can make it easier to seek out help in the future too. This allows us to set aside our fear of having a dependence on someone else or looking like we might appear weak in the eyes of others. At the end of the day, it's all about achieving what you want out of life, while continuing to discover new ways to let go of the fears that hold us back.

It is important to note that not all fears are necessarily bad for us. Some of the things we are most afraid of—such as a fear of heights or drowning—are actually natural self-preservation instincts meant to keep us from harm. While we can learn to control those types of fears, completely eliminating them may not always be in our best interest. And since we don't tend to encounter these situations on a daily basis, they usually don't have much of an impact on our lives.

On the other hand, the anxiety-inducing fears that keep us from achieving our goals are things that we not only need to address but learn to let go of completely. When we take the necessary steps to conquer those fears, we can start to live a more fear-free life, allowing us to move forward with confidence and conviction in everything we do.

Which brings us back to the first real step in letting go of our fears—properly identifying exactly what those fears are. The truth is, most of us don't have a fear of heights; instead we have a fear of falling from a tall place and getting injured when we hit the ground. Similarly, giving a speech to a large crowd isn't what really scares us either; it's getting up in front of a group of strangers and looking like we're unprepared or lacking in knowledge. When we've reached a point where we can be honest with ourselves about where our true fears truly lie, we can finally begin to let them go for good.

With the root of your fear properly identified you can start to examine exactly why that fear has such a strong hold on you. Is there a real, tangible danger that you are right to be frightened of or is it something more irrational in nature? Is it grounded in reality or is it simply uncertainty generated from within your brain?

In a lot of ways, the more tangible fears—like a fear of snakes or heights—are much easier to deal with and ultimately let go. While an encounter with a snake can be terrifying, most of us don't encounter those creatures on a regular basis, allowing us to go on with our lives without worry.

On the other hand, our inner fears can be much more difficult to let go, simply because they come from a place inside of us that is not always rational or easy to identify. Those are the fears that we need to get more familiar with in order to help us understand them better. In doing so, we can push ourselves to confront them directly and work to overcome them once and for all.

In order to do that, however, we have to actively work at putting those fears behind us forever. That means not ignoring them, but instead embracing the things that frighten us the most and looking for ways to get past them. By not confronting our phobias we are allowing them to linger and grow, which means that they will continue to have a hold on us. But by actively working to get past them we can learn much more about ourselves too, giving us the self-assurance we need to let go of them forever.

At first glance, the basic tools you need to finally release your fears may seem too simple to be effective. But the reality is that many of the things that frighten us the most come from feelings of uncertainty and doubt in our own abilities. By focusing on turning our micro-goals into micro-successes, we can start to build confidence within ourselves, which takes away much of the power that our fears hold over us. Once that happens, we can step up to take on more ambitious challenges knowing that we are capable of achieving things that were once out of reach.

Letting go of your fears can be an incredibly liberating feeling, like a tremendous weight being removed from your shoulders. In doing so, you're not just releasing the shackles that have held you in place for so long, you're giving yourself permission to believe that you can accomplish anything that you set your mind to. When that happens, you've truly unlocked one of the keys to leading a completely successful life, no matter where your path takes you.

Don't allow fear to keep you from living the life you want to lead. By taking the bold step of facing down your fears, your courage and trust in yourself will grow to new levels, taking you to places that you've only imagined. Be bold and trust in yourself and your goals will never be out of reach.